Laughter and Tears

Laughter and Tears

Donald Proffitt

THE PENTLAND PRESS LTD.
EDINBURGH · CAMBRIDGE · DURHAM

First published in 1992 by
The Pentland Press Ltd.
5 Hutton Close
South Church
Bishop Auckland
Durham

ISBN 1872795 84 6

Typeset by Spire Origination Ltd., Norwich
Printed and bound by Antony Rowe Ltd., Chippenham

This book I dedicate to my wife, Loïs, as a small token of my very sincere thanks and appreciation for all that she has done for me, our children and grandchildren, over many years – in fact, at the end of 1992, it will be our Golden Wedding Anniversary.

The depth of darkness into which you can descend and still live, is an exact measure, I believe, of the height to which you can aspire to reach.

Author unknown

Contents

Introduction

A number of my friends have asked me when I began to contemplate 'writing', what made me do it and whether anything lies behind these efforts? They are not easy questions to answer, but as I have always believed one should try to be self-analytical, so I have attempted, in this introduction, to give some of the reasons.

I have always been fascinated by the written and the spoken word. This stems, perhaps, from school-days, when I had as one of my teachers, for Greek and Latin, a most remarkable gentleman — Mr. C. V. Merritt. An Old Boy of the school said, when he heard of C. V. M.'s death a few years ago, '. . . he taught and required a rare standard of impeccable scholarship in the classic definition of grammar.' In his honour I relate one of his poems:-

Evening

The hour when pale-winged mists with cool embrace
Enfold the plain and kiss the sleeping hills;
When beast and bird are hushed, and laughing rills
Seem somehow, though not lessening their pace,
To laugh more softly; when to hide their face,
The night-shy daisies fold their red-tipt frills,
While honeysuckle sweetlier distils
Its stored ambrosia for th'ephemeral race
Of moths to spoil — that blessed evening hour,
Time of tranquillity, what wondrous power
Is hers to soothe the vexed day-weary mind!
So, when the hot noonday of life shall cease
And the long afternoon be left behind,
Still may the evening of my days bring peace!

As one grows older it is natural, I suppose, to think more of the past and rather less of the future, without entirely forgetting the latter. In Rhosneigr, on Anglesey, where we have taken holidays for 45 years, I began to remember, as I walked alone along the lovely beaches there, many family incidents and hence *Random Recollections*. The name of our house is Random! It was my first real attempt to write a poem, in July 1988. I thought also of my time in the R.A.F. during the last war and that brought to mind the sensitive verse, written by Pilot Officer John Gillespie Magee, which I present to you here:-

Oh, I have slipped the surly bonds of earth
And danced the skies on laughter-silvered wings;
Sunward I've climbed, and joined the tumbling mirth
Of sun-split clouds — and done a hundred things
You have not dreamed of — wheeled and soared and swung
High in the sunlit silence. Hov'ring there,
I've chased the shouting wind along, and flung
My eager craft through footless halls of air.
Up, up the long, delirious, burning blue
I've topped the windswept heights with easy grace
Where never lark, nor even eagle flew.
And, while with silent, lifting mind I've trod
The high untrespassed sanctity of space,
Put out my hand, and touched the face of God.

My father was in the R.F.C. in the 1914–18 war. I recalled some of the verses that he and I had chatted about and sorted out — and that is now 60 years ago!

I also recollected upon the hard-working, but very happy days that resulted from a link-up with my father-in-law in 1947, when I helped to build, from scratch, a family firm which became a public company. Many times he said to his friends in Liverpool, 'Well I had to get a "proffitt" into the business somehow!' After a few laughs he would add, 'Even if he turns out to be a dead loss, in the end!'

It was tough; a seven day week; utter dedication to creating something that eventually gave employment to 600 people; trying to provide sound products, well-presented and fulfilling the customers' needs — and we had a lot of fun too.

I also dwelt upon "Man's inhumanity to Man" and the need for us all to act in a more responsible way towards one another, and the complaining that goes on when most people in this country are so much better off than millions of our fellow men and women in other parts of the world.

I have been fortunate in having a deep involvement for 15 years in the gardening and forestry industries. This has brought home very forcibly the beauty of plants and trees, the importance we should all attach to our environment and the duty we have towards our descendants in this matter. Those people employed in, or running such businesses, are so friendly, helpful and dedicated, that it makes one wonder whether the products they deal with somehow influence the human mind and outlook on life.

I believe that, in the short period of years we are given, we should set our sights high in everything that we undertake and I do not mean in a selfish way. We should allow ourselves time to dream, but not then to ignore totally harsh reality. We should have some enjoyment and fun, providing that there is a serious understanding of our duties to others. Most important of all do the best we can to help, to advise and to guide, when required, our children and grand-children.

I hope that I may have answered the questions set out at the beginning of this introduction. It seems rather strange, in a way, that what sparked off all my thoughts, which undoubtedly I had had at the back of my brain for some time — and put them, over a short period, into written form — was the discovery of that lovely undamaged shell on Broad Beach at Rhosneigr as mentioned in *Random Recollections*. How often, I wonder, does Nature act as a catalyst to encourage Man to undertake projects, including inventions, that may have been hidden dreams, tucked away in the mind?

Donald Proffitt.

FAMILY AND FRIENDS

'Random' Recollections

I saw a conch upon Broad Beach
And thought, I'll take it back to teach
The grandchildren, how they,
When in their homes, or far away,
Could still recall the whisp'ring sea
In Rhosneigr on Anglesey,
By quietly listening to the sound
Within a shell, like Grandpa found.

For Granny and me what fun and games
We had with Jonathan and James,
And recollections stick
Of Camilla, Lucy and Patrick,
Hannah, Jeremy as well,
Amanda, Nicholas and Samuel —
The last two still to come
And stay with us at 'Random'.

So many memories to cheer
And bring a smile, sometimes a tear.
The little things we've loved and those
Seem yet more precious as one grows
Older and thinks upon the past
And counts one's blessings while they last.
Of holidays which still stay clear,
Our children growing year by year.

To recall big games of rummy
And surfing flat upon your tummy
And kick-the-can and Mrs. Jones,
With glaring eyes and strident tones
Saying, 'What is all that noise' —
In fact she loved the girls and boys —
And crashing seas on Lion Rock.
I wish I could turn back the clock.

And rounders with loud yells and cries
And lovely sunsets in evening skies
And buckets full of shrimps for tea
And rambling round the lake to see
How many wild birds could be found —
And so one's thoughts go round and round —
And climbing Snowdon, water-skis,
'Another pony ride, oh please!'

And building castles on the shore
And, 'Can't we go in just once more?'
They said, 'The sea's so warm and nice.'
And older folk did not think twice!
Oh, how have all the years gone by
So quickly, and you wonder why
The bad times fade, the good you keep,
So warming, 'til your final sleep.

Christmas 1990

What a joyous time for Granny and me,
Staying with Susie and her family.
Lots of giggling with Amanda and James
And then puzzling out some difficult games.
Tony, quite determined to land his 'plane,
Even if it meant trying again (and again)!
And Susie providing the overall touch
Of everything wanted. We thank you so much.

Then off to Gillie's — a marvellous scene,
Paul frantically busy with his *haute cuisine*.
Lovely flowers and the Christmas tree,
With presents as far as the eye could see.
Jonathan, sadly, not feeling too good,
So unable to pile in to the glorious food
And Hannah as usual bursting with joy
And Patrick like a colourful Indian boy.

Next, turkey and hats and crackers and wine
And the brandy-lit pudding was simply divine.
Afterwards, of course, we 'phoned several others,
Not forgetting those two absent brothers.
We got through to Toby in distant Tangier,
As we wanted to wish him a happy New Year.
Now it's all over with much to remember,
So what's going to happen next December?

A Past Thought

Why did I suddenly think of her,
As I walked along that West Indian beach?
It all happened fifty years ago
And yet it stays so very clear.
The war was twelve months on and
I had only reached a score of birthdays,
When she appeared and changed my life.
The very first girl-friend — what a joke today —
And there were lots of tears
When I was posted many miles away.
Then in January '41, when I was twenty-one,
I received a little poem from her
Which I can still remember —

As the mingling colours of the evening sky,
As the leaves brown rustle as the wind goes by,
As the waves rough crash on a rocky shore,
Such is my love for you and more.

More than the love of man for man,
More than human thought can span,
But vast as the stars and the moon above,
So do I care for you my love.

And though we may be lands apart,
Your touch is locked within my heart
Locked around with memories sweet
To cheer me 'til the day we meet.

However, she sent back the engagement ring,
Saying we were too young and she had
Ambition to succeed within the W.A.A.F.
As it turned out she was right. The pain
Was agonising at the time, but life
Moved on and though I saw her once again
By then, I had found my future wife.

Experiences like these do bite so deep
That always in your heart you keep
Them and they never completely fade away.
So that, I suppose, was why I thought of her upon that sunny day.

'Yes Darling, Grandpa has gone for his walk to Lion Rock'

Memories flooded in. The sea, gently sifting the shingly-sand seemed to say, 'Stay with us'. As the sun went down his life slipped quietly away. 'So sad,' they said, when they found him sitting in lonely silence and wept, wondering at the serene smile on the dead man's face.

In Loving Memory of Pete Jones

Old Pete has died. I'm so upset.
For many years he helped me to get
My garden looking rather good.
As he grew older then he should
Have taken things a shade more quiet.
Instead he produced the daily diet
For his two sons. He used to like his beer,
So the pubs will miss him much round here.
He cleaned the house, did the shopping,
Washed the clothes and then was hopping
Around his vegetable patch.
There are very few to-day who match
His conscientious way of life
And now he's gone to join his wife.
My thoughts of you will never cease,
God bless you Pete — go rest in peace.

From the Heart

Flowers arrived as I lay in that hospital bed
And I have to admit that a few tears were shed.
This illness has shown the great depth of thought
That my wife and children and grandchildren have brought
To this totally unexpected and unpleasant upset.
For what they have done, I will never forget.

HUMOUR

The Residence Constructed by John (or The House that Jack Built)

This is the gallinaceous biped,
Whose matutinal ejaculations awoke from his somnolent repose
The cropped and beardless ecclesiastic,
Who united in the bonds of holy matrimony
The individual of the dilapidated habiliments
To the lone and disconsolate virgin,
Who extracted the lactic fluid
From the female bovine creature,
Who projected to an altitude the canine quadruped,
Who disturbed the equanimity of the feline domesticated creature,
Who assassinated the obnoxious vermin dwelling
In the domiciliary edifice erected by John.

Who — What — Where!

Down came his sleeves rolled up,
Off came his coat on.
He missed the tram he came upon.
If he doesn't come now he is sure to.
If he does he mightn't.

Roundabout

One fine October's morning
In August, last July,
The sun lay thick upon the ground,
The snow shone in the sky.
The flowers were busy nesting,
The birds were all in bloom,
As I went down the cellar
To clean the upstairs room.
I saw a thousand miles ahead
A house alone, between two more.
Its front door was at the back
And all its walls were whitewashed black.

Go Diva!

They had an awful row. She rather fancied her powerful voice. 'You can see I have nothing to wear!' she yelled. 'Get off your high horse, or depart!' he shouted. 'Cease taxing me!' she bridled and rode into the town, combing her long flowing locks. The citizenry averted their gaze.

CONTEMPLATION

Hell or Heaven

How pathetically insignificant is Man
And what makes this comment even worse,
Is the pontificating cant that tries to show
He's master of the universe.

Consider the environmental problems with which we are now
   faced
And, just think, he cannot even properly care,
Within his tiny home, the earth,
For the land and sea and air.

It sometimes seems that the only motivating themes of life
Are the pursuit of power and glory,
But unless Man can really face the years that lie ahead
Then time, undoubtedly, will tell a different story.

How utterly repugnant that religion features so strongly in
   human conflict.
Where is the patience that should be ever there
And shown to all one's fellow men and women,
Whatever colour, race and creed they bear?

Perhaps, one day, some world-wide cataclysmic act of nature
Will show to all Mankind a real Hell.
Then maybe everyone who stays alive
Will together make the earth a better place in which to dwell.

So Little Time . . .

You have to strive to stay alive
To make your dreams come true.
Not every one, that could be bad,
But those achieved can make you glad
That you have seen them through.

However, you must count the cost
Of setting sights so high
And wonder whether you have been
A little selfish, sometimes mean,
In pitching for the sky.

How many people have you helped
Make life a shade more bright?
How often paused to give some thought
To fresh fields that you sought,
But then gave in to someone else's right?

So little time for all those things
That mean so much to you to hear,
Or feel, or see — perhaps
Some may forgive the occasional lapse
Of thanks that did not appear.

For suddenly you realise, at three score years and ten,
That time is running out.
So what of all those many dreams
You've not achieved? Now it seems
It's memories to think about.

There are some, maybe years ago,
You cannot quite forget,
No matter how you try.
Perhaps they're not important, yet
They still can make you cry.

'These I have loved', the poet said
And if you think, you'll find
That you have also much to treasure,
The little things that gave such pleasure,
And stay within your mind.

And so you should give heartfelt thanks
For the blessings of your life,
For children and their laughter
And grandchildren coming after
And the patience of your wife.

Rest Content

Never to see again the glorious changing colours of the sky at
   night,
The splendour of mighty snow-clad hills,
Or the beauty of a rose.

Never to hear again the thrilling music and the poignant arias in
   opera,
The laughter of little children,
Or the songs of birds at dawn.

Never to taste again delicious home-made pies and cakes and
   bread,
Scones and strawberry jam and cream,
Or vegetables, garden-grown.

Never to smell again new-mown grass that makes you think of
   playing-fields at school,
The scent of multi-coloured sweet peas,
Or coffee newly-ground.

Never to feel again the tingling freshness when you're back from
   winter walks,
The crispness of linen sheets upon your bed,
Or the softness of a woman's lips.

Never to sense again unspoken love and the comfort of old
   friendships,
The pleasure of giving unrequested help,
Or the joy of living free.

But, if you've had the good fortune to experience all of these —
And probably many more, if you carefully recollect —
Why then life owes you nought.

So go to your rest content.

A Dying Wish

When I die there will, I suppose, be tears.
My wife and family thinking of the many years
We spent together. The memories, so wonderfully good,
Will, I am sure, remain; but it seems to me it would
Be better if there was no lingering sorrow,
But rather that most thoughts should be about tomorrow.
Our grandchildren, unfortunately, will face
A changing world, that clearly has a much too rapid pace
Of so-called progress. It will be difficult to retain
High standards of behaviour and maintain
A civilised attitude towards one's fellow men
And women. So may I ask you then
To always carry with you and apply them everywhere
The words Respect and Honesty, Forgiveness and Care.
Oh, by the way, I hope that when I go,
The service will include that Intermezzo!

Nature's Way of Life

A full moon rose up in the clear-sky night,
Spreading all round blue ethereal light.
After some minutes I was able to see,
Sitting alone 'neath a nearby tree
A quiet busy-nibbling little hare.
Suddenly he sat up, for he had spotted there
A slinking fox, who arrived just too late
To collect the supper for his cubs and mate.
Then I detected upon a high bough
A large contemplative owl — I suppose wondering how
He could quickly discover a succulent mouse
To take back home to his nearby house.
Cruel? But that has always been the same,
The way Nature plays a continuing game.
Man does not need to go on killing
His fellow beings who are not willing
To follow him, come what may.
All hope to carry on day by day
To make their families happy, healthy
And very few say, 'I must be wealthy'.
It is intolerance and utter selfish greed
That causes Man upon his fellow men to feed
His totally uncaring ambition for big ME;
But Nature will take over eventually
And Man will disappear without any trace,
The world continuing with its natural face.

To Climb a Mountain

The last few metres were an agonising struggle. At the top he fell, sobbing with pain, his breath coming in unsteady gasps. Suddenly the misty clouds which had covered the mountain for much of the day fleetingly cleared away. He slowly dragged himself to his feet, gazing in awe and wonder at the incredible snow-clad scene around him. A faint smile crossed his tired face. Slowly, his knees buckling, he collapsed to the ground. He slid a hand into his jacket pocket making sure the letter was there and then slowly he pulled it out. As his eyes closed for the last time he whispered ever so faintly, 'My darling Rosie.'

'C'est pas possible' said Jean-Claude angrily and Henri, turning to the bar, grunted, 'Tu es fou.'

'Look Harry, can't you persuade Roger that climbing up there on his own is a bit daft?' said George, 'After all you are a doctor and . . . .'

'Don't worry about me, George', broke in Roger, 'I have always wanted to do this, it's a . . . . oh, I don't know, it's just something I have to do before . . . .' and then he broke off.

'Avant quoi?' Henri growled.

'Before I get as old and ugly and grumpy as you,' Roger quickly retorted. Everyone grinned, including Henri and then they all looked at Harry. A quiet thoughtful man, who always took his time over replying to any question, he murmured, 'Well it's up to Roger. It's his life. He's a good climber and knows the risks. The weather forecast is not that good for the next couple of days so maybe he will sleep on it and think again.' Roger smiled. He and Harry looked steadily into one another's eyes as the others began to talk about climbing.

It had been rather a late night. Roger had excused himself and gone off to bed early. The telephone ringing loudly by his bed made Harry jump wondering for a moment where he was. When he picked up the receiver he heard a somewhat anxious voice saying, 'Harry, is that you? It's Rosemary here.' He quickly sat upright, noting that it was 10 a.m. 'I am sorry if I woke you but I have been trying to get Roger — there's no answer. What's happened to him? Is he O.K.? You see I . . .' and then Harry could hear her crying.

'Rosemary — calm down my dear. Roger's fine. He didn't stay up late last night so he's probably gone for an early morning walk — you know what he's like for fresh air and . . .' It was difficult keeping up this line, but Rosemary broke in, 'What I was going to say, Harry, was I have a feeling something is not quite right. He has been so sweet to me over the past few months and I know he has been looking forward to this climbing trip with you and his pals. He's had a funny look in his eyes and . . . oh Harry, I really am worried. I don't know why.'

Harry quietly said, 'Rosemary we'll 'phone you later. We should have been out by now, but the weather looks as though it's closed down a bit so I am not quite sure what we will be doing, but please cheer up and I will tell Roger you called.' He heard a click as the telephone was put down at the other end of the line and instinctively knew he had not entirely convinced her about her beloved husband.

Two days later they found him on the mountain-top. There was no need to check really but Jean-Claude quietly said, 'You had better take a look, Harry.'

27

'He's gone, I'm afraid,' replied Harry. George slowly withdrew the envelope from the lifeless hand that held it and said in a bright voice that was desperately trying to cover up his sorrow, 'It's addressed to our doctor friend and his pals.'

Harry opened it and read, 'My dear Harry. I don't know if I'll do it, but I am bloody well going to try. It will be my last chance and you will be aware of how much it means to me to achieve this goal.'

As Harry paused for a moment, Henri, gruffly and with tears in his eyes, interrupted and said, 'Qu'est ce qu'il dit?'

Harry continued, 'We all have to set ourselves targets, or have dreams or aspirations and there comes a time when — I had better stop rabbiting on Harry. Thank you, my dear old friend, for all your help and for keeping our secret. Tell the lads if you wish and Rosie and please keep an eye on her for me and give her the other letter which I have enclosed. God bless you all — Roger. . . . P.S. If I get to the top I would like to stay there if possible to save everyone a lot of trouble now and later.'

Harry turned away, the others waiting in silence. Then he said, 'You see Roger had a terminal condition. Last year I said that he probably had maybe three or four months left. He didn't want anyone to know about it, even his wife. "Why worry other people?" he said to me, "I'm not going out with a whimper. I've got to climb that mountain on my own and go out joyful."'

They made a cairn to cover him. No-one said much and then only in quiet tones. When they had finished they all slowly trudged away, Harry being the last to leave. He would never know why he had brought the two pieces of wood with him. They made a small cross upon which was merely written — 'Roger'.

POSTSCRIPT

Think Big

If you think you are beaten, you are,
If you think you dare not, you daren't,
If you'd like to win, but you think you can't
It's almost a cinch you won't.
If you think you'll lose, you're lost
For out in the world you'll find
Success begins with a fellow's will —
It's all in the state of the mind.

Full many a race is lost
'Ere ever a step is run,
And many a coward fails
'Ere ever his work's begun.
Think big and your deeds will grow,
Think small and you'll fall behind,
Think that you can and you will,
It's all in the state of the mind.

If you think you're outclassed you are,
You've got to think high to rise.
You've got to be sure of yourself, before
You can ever win a prize.
Life's battles don't always go
To the stronger or faster man,
But soon or late the man who wins
Is the fellow who thinks he can.

Source unknown